IN HIS HANDS

IN HIS HANDS

A Daily Devotional for the NICU Journey

Erin Amyx

Copyright © 2025 Erin Amyx
All rights reserved.
Cover Art by Ashley Bordelon
ISBN 13: 9798307932902
All Scripture quotations, unless otherwise indicated are taken from the Holy Bible, New International Version®, NIV®. Copyright© 1973,1978,1984,2011 by Biblica, Inc.™ Used by permission of Zondervan. All rights reserved worldwide www.zondervan.com The "NIV" and "New International Version" are trademarks registered in the United States Patent and Trademark Office by Biblica, Inc.™

Scripture quotations are from the ESV ® Bible (The Holy Bible, English Standard Version ®), © 2001 by Crossway, a publishing ministry of Good News Publishers. Used by permission. All rights reserved. The ESV text may not be quoted in any publication made available to the public by a Creative Commons license. The ESV may not be translated in whole or in part in any other language.

ACKNOWLEDGEMENTS

Thank you to Mrs. Emily and my sister-in-law, Adrien, for helping me edit my work.

Thank you Ashley Bordelon, a fellow NICU mom, for the beautiful cover art.

Thank you to my parents for editing, giving me ideas, and encouraging me when I doubted myself.

Last but not least, thank you to my husband for editing, giving me ideas, putting up with me, always encouraging me, and for everything you did with the kids and around the house while I wrote.

Introduction

Hi! My name is Erin. I wanted to introduce myself before I start to pray with you. I'm a wife and a mom of two beautiful daughters as I write this. My first daughter was born full term with a basically textbook pregnancy and delivery. My second however, was very different. I found out at about 20 weeks pregnant that I had a placenta accreta, so we were watching that closely. Then, around 26 weeks pregnant, I started bleeding and was told it was "normal for an accreta". At 27&3 I went to L&D for bleeding that just didn't feel right. I was flown from central Louisiana to Texas Children's Hospital in Houston, TX and was told they were prepared to do a c-section in the air if needed. Thankfully that didn't happen, and I had my baby at 27&5 due to a partial placental abruption. We spent 80 days in the NICU, 300 miles from home. You'll learn more as we pray together, but I wanted to give you an intro as to why I felt led to write this devotional. I'm equally so happy and so sorry that you're here. You reading this book likely means that you have a NICU baby yourself. If that's the case, I'm so glad this found you. If not, thank you for praying with us anyway.

Every NICU journey is different, and you may come across some devotions that don't pertain to you. That's okay! Use these days to pray for the people around you who may be going through these things.

I tried to keep each day short because I know how hard it can be to focus while in the NICU. You'll notice a journaling section beside each devotion. Use this for whatever you'd like! Write anything you think of while reading the devotional. Add the date and maybe write baby's weight and something the doctors said today. Write questions you have for the doctors, so you don't forget. Keep track of the milestones your baby has met already! It's your book! Use it however you'd like.

THOUGHTS FOR TODAY

DAY 1

2 Samuel 12:23 NIV But now that he is gone, why should I go on fasting? Can I bring him back again? I will go to him, but he will not return to me.

Mark 10:16 And He took the children in His arms, placed His hands on them and blessed them.

He's got all the angel babies in His hands. The babies that have gone to be with Jesus. Whether these babies were born into His arms, or they fought here on Earth before going to the Lord, He is holding them now. If there is anything that could possibly give you peace, let it be that the Lord, our Savior, is holding your sweet baby in His arms. I'm so sorry for your loss.

Dear Lord, we know that you are holding the sweet angel babies in Your hands. You are holding the angel babies' parents as well. Hold them as they grieve. Give them a sense of peace that only You can provide. In Your name we pray, Amen.

THOUGHTS FOR TODAY

DAY 2

Deuteronomy 31:6 Be strong and courageous. Do not be afraid or terrified because of them, for the Lord your God goes with you; He will never leave nor forsake you.

He's got the mom who is SO strong in His hands. The mama who is learning just how strong she really is. This mama has gone through so much in a short amount of time. I never knew how strong I could be until they told me at 27 weeks pregnant that I was about to have a baby. When I looked in her isolette and saw my little fighter, I knew I needed to try and be just as strong as she was.

Dear Lord, we pray for the mama who is learning her own strength in a way she never would've imagined. We pray that You will be with her throughout her journey and help renew her strength when she finds herself struggling. May she know that You are always with her. In Your name we pray, Amen.

THOUGHTS FOR TODAY

DAY 3

Psalm 103:13 As a father has compassion on his children, so the Lord has compassion on those who fear Him.

He's got the dad who can't physically be there in His hands. Whether dad has to work, or he is hundreds of miles away, this dad wants so badly to be there for his family. He'd give anything to hold that baby and mama in his arms today. In a lot of situations, since mom is the main food source for baby, if someone has to go back to work, it is going to be Dad. We were 300 miles from home during our NICU journey. My husband's job was amazing and let him off for 3 weeks and he could leave at the drop of a hat if needed. The rest of the time, he could only come to Houston on the weekends. I was so thankful for his sacrifice to continue providing for our family.

Dear Lord, thank You for the dads that long to be present. They wish they could be there holding their family, but they know they need to work to provide for them. Give them peace in knowing that You have the whole family in Your hands and have this all under control. Help this dad to rest in You. In Your name we pray, Amen.

THOUGHTS FOR TODAY

DAY 4

Jeremiah 17:14 Heal me, Lord, and I will be healed; save me and I will be saved.

He's got the mama who's still healing in His hands. This mama is still healing herself and is trying to take care of her NICU baby too. Healing from birth is hard enough in itself. Healing from a likely traumatic birth while worrying about your NICU baby is even harder. Let yourself heal and rest.

Dear Lord, we pray for the mama who is still healing from her birth. Whether vaginal or c-section, an early delivery is never easy-physically or emotionally. Heal this mama's body and multiply her rest so she can recover and care for her sweet baby. In Your name we pray, Amen.

THOUGHTS FOR TODAY

DAY 5

Ecclesiastes 11:5 As you do not know the path of the wind, or how the body is formed in a mother's womb, so you cannot understand the work of God, the Maker of all things.

He's got the little bitty babies in His hands. The nano and micro-preemies. The babies wearing the smallest diapers you've ever seen. These babies are small but mighty! My baby was born at 27 weeks and was thankfully big for her gestational age-2 pounds and 12 ounces. I'm thankful that she was so big, but to me, she was still so tiny. God helped her little body fight as hard as she could, and He is helping your baby too. God is helping your baby fight whether they are under a pound or twelve pounds. Pray with me for strength for your tiny fighter.

Dear Lord, the NICU is full of babies big and small. Right now, we pray for their strength. Strength to fight through the bradys. Strength to fight their infections. Strength during surgery. Strength to heal the brain bleeds. Strength to breathe and eat without interventions. Lord, we pray that You will make these babies strong as well as their mamas. Be with these families today. In Your name we pray, Amen.

THOUGHTS FOR TODAY

DAY 6

1 Thessalonians 2:7-8a Instead, we were like young children among you. Just as a nursing mother cares for her children, so we cared for you

He's got the mama who is pumping in His hands. Woooo! Pumping! Every 2 to 4 hours for 15 to 30 minutes. Where does the time go? Once you finish pumping, wash your pump parts, bottle the milk, maybe bring it to the milk bank, it's time to pump again. Don't even get me started on waking up at night to pump! Feeding your baby with your body is an amazing thing. AND (not but) it is oh so tiring. Let's pray for rest today.

Dear Lord, this mama is feeding her baby with her body. How amazing is that? Thank You for blessing us with the ability to do so. It is such a blessing to be able to do this AND it can be exhausting. Stretch this mama's rest tonight. Help her mind and body to recover from what she's going through. In Your name we pray, Amen.

THOUGHTS FOR TODAY

DAY 7

Hebrews 13:1 Keep on loving one another as brothers and sisters.

He's got all the big siblings in His hands. Having older kids at home, no matter their age, is hard. It's hard on the parents but it's also so hard on the kids. Younger kids are confused why you're gone so much and older kids have more of an understanding of what's going on. My NICU journey was 300 miles away with an almost 3 year old at home. She stayed with me in Houston for a week at a time, and a week at home with dad, who had to work. It was so hard on her being away, knowing something was wrong. She was too young to understand but old enough to know something was up. Today, let's pray for strength and understanding for these awesome big siblings.

Dear Lord, siblings are always such a blessing to a baby. When a NICU journey is involved, it gets more complicated. They don't understand. We pray for their strength while mom and dad are with baby and understanding that fits their knowledge. We pray for the parents who feel guilty while splitting their time. May they know that You have them right where they need to be. We thank You for this little family You've blessed us with. In Your name we pray, Amen.

THOUGHTS FOR TODAY

DAY 8

Philippians 4:6 Do not be anxious about anything, but in every situation, by prayer and petition with thanksgiving, present your requests to God.

He's got the monitor watching mama in His hands. It's so hard to pull your eyes away from those monitors. Waiting to see if they are about to go off. Looking to see when the last alarm was. How low was the last Brady? When was the last time they stopped breathing? I remember being there. The nurses would get on to me and turn the monitor so I couldn't watch it so much because I "couldn't take it home with me". It's time for you to breathe mama. He's got you and your baby in His hands and has it all under control.

Dear Lord, those monitors are both a blessing and a curse. It's good to see how your baby is doing but it can also cause so much anxiety. Please remind us that there is no need to be anxious. Instead, let us turn to You in prayer. You've got this. Give these mamas peace and rest today. In Your name we pray, Amen.

THOUGHTS FOR TODAY

DAY 9

Matthew 14:14 When Jesus landed and saw a large crowd, he had compassion on them and healed their sick.

He's got the sepsis work up baby in His hands. Blood, urine, spinal tap-oh my! Sepsis workups are the worst! They are so scary. My baby had three in the 80 days we were there. They're so hard on the baby. It always broke my heart. Thankfully all of hers were negative! I pray yours are too.

Dear Lord, we pray for the babies going through sepsis work ups. Give them strength to tolerate the work up. There must be something going on for the work up to be happening Lord. So we pray You'll heal their little body of whatever is hurting them and help them to continue to fight. In Your name we pray, Amen.

THOUGHTS FOR TODAY

DAY 10

2 Corinthians 8:7 So whether we are at home or away, we make it our aim to please him.

He's got the far from home mama in His hands. This mama may be commuting hours a day to see her baby in the NICU. Or she may be like me and home is too far to drive every day. We were so blessed to rent a condo a mile from the hospital for the 3 months we were there because home was 5 hours away. Maybe this mama is in a Ronald McDonald House every night, so she can be close to baby. Let's pray for these mamas.

Dear Lord, there are mamas today who are far from home so they can be with their baby. These mamas are strong! We thank you for making it possible for them to stay. Lord, we pray that You'll continue to bless them with whatever resources they need to stay close to baby as long as needed. In Your name we pray, Amen.

THOUGHTS FOR TODAY

DAY 11

Romans 8:28 And we know that in all things God works for the good of those who love Him, who have been called according to His purpose.

He's got the doctors and the nurses in His hands. The people in charge of our babies' care. I hope you have that favorite nurse and maybe a favorite doctor that you think about while reading this. We sure did! Haley, Elizabeth, Taylor, Jamal, Rachel and Meg were our favorite nurses (I couldn't pick just one, okay?!) and we'll call our favorite doctor, Dr. B. Good doctors and nurses can really change the course of a day, week, or entire NICU journey.

Dear Lord, we thank You for the medical professionals that care for our babies! We pray that You will guide their decisions and their hands while working with them. I pray these mamas have the best doctors and nurses out there. I pray You'll give this mama the strength and courage to advocate for her baby no matter what. In Your name we pray, Amen.

THOUGHTS FOR TODAY

Day 12

Isaiah 41:10 So do not fear, for I am with you; do not be dismayed, for I am your God. I will strengthen you and help you; I will uphold you with my righteous right hand.

He's got the mom who blames herself in His hands. The mom who thinks somehow her baby needing the NICU is her fault. The mom who thinks she caused this to happen. I was this mom. I had a placental abruption at 27 weeks. I can't think of a single thing that could've caused the abruption, but in my brain, it was my fault. Now, I know better.

Dear Lord, comfort this mama and assure her that this is all in Your plan. Nothing surprises You Lord, and I think we forget that. Give this mama peace knowing that she didn't do anything to cause this for her sweet baby. In Your name we pray, Amen.

THOUGHTS FOR TODAY

DAY 13

Jeremiah 29:11 "For I know the plans I have for you," declares the Lord, "plans to prosper you and not to harm you, plans to give you hope and a future"

He's got your uncertain future in His hands. To Him, your future is anything but uncertain. He knows every step your baby will take in life. He knows the plans He has for you and your baby and has it all laid out perfectly. Try not to worry about what is to come, because it is all in His hands.

Dear Lord, this mama is worried about her baby's future, but You are not. You know everything that will happen, and it is all for Your glory. Let this mama rest knowing that Your plans are to prosper and not to harm. Give her hope, Lord. In Your name we pray, Amen.

THOUGHTS FOR TODAY

DAY 14

Psalms 127:3-5 Children are a heritage from the Lord, offspring a reward from Him. Like arrows in the hands of a warrior are children born in one's youth. Blessed is the man whose quiver is full of them. They will not be put to shame when they contend with their opponents in court.

He's got the mama of many in his hands. The mama with other kids at home. It's so hard to split your time! I was away from home and had my older daughter a week at a time usually. But I imagine that being close to home and leaving your kids daily to see your baby is a different kind of hard. And still having supper to cook, baths to give, and bedtime to tend to on top of your NICU journey. I can't imagine. Let's pray for these mamas.

Dear Lord, today we pray for the mama whose quiver is full. The mama who has kids waiting at home when she leaves the NICU. Kids that she leaves at home or brings to school when going to see baby. This mama is superhuman. Juggling a NICU journey with everyday life. Help her to rest tonight between everyone leaning on her. In Your name we pray, Amen.

THOUGHTS FOR TODAY

DAY 15

Proverbs 17:6 Children's children are a crown to the aged and parents are the pride of their children.

He's got all the loving grandparents in his hands. Having your parents to help during this difficult time is priceless. It can be easy to forget that this may be hard for them as well. They want to take care of their babies as well. I was so thankful for my parents and in-laws during our NICU journey. My in-laws kept things running at home including getting the nursery ready and deep cleaning our house. My mom stayed in Houston with me, which was so good for me mentally, especially during the weeks that my older daughter was there. My dad, like my husband, had to work and was there as much as he could be. Let's pray for the loving, helpful grandparents in these journeys with us.

Dear Lord, we are so thankful for the grandparents you blessed our babies with. I know some of us couldn't get through this without them. Give them the strength to get through this and the understanding they need to know how to help their kids through one of the hardest times of their lives. In Your name we pray, Amen.

THOUGHTS FOR TODAY

DAY 16

2 Chronicles 20:17a "You will not have to fight this battle. Take up your positions; stand firm and see the deliverance the Lord will give you"

He's got the advocating mama in His hands. This mama is on fire fighting for her baby. She knows her baby and advocates for everything they need. Sometimes it can be intimidating to stand up to a team of doctors and voice your opinion, but you've got this. No one can fight for your baby like you. Our hardest day in the NICU was one that I had to fight for my baby. I knew she needed blood, and she ended up back on the CPAP before someone would listen to me. Sure enough, I was right. She received two units of blood and was almost immediately able to come back off CPAP. Mama knows her baby the best! Don't doubt that.

Dear Lord, You put a fiery spirit in this mama so she can advocate for her little love. We ask that You give her the courage to do it, and that You will guide her words as she speaks to the doctors. In Your name we pray, Amen.

THOUGHTS FOR TODAY

DAY 17

2 Timothy 1:7 For God has not given us a spirit of fear but of power, love, and sound judgement.

He's got the baby who needs surgery in His hands. This baby may be having surgery today or not for another month. Either way, the thought of this surgery is heavy on these parents minds. Try not to worry, God has your baby and their surgeons in His hands and is ready to guide them through it.

Dear Lord, You did not give these parents a spirit of fear, but one of power and love. May they come to You through the power of prayer and place their worries in Your hands. Give them peace in knowing that even if they are afraid, You are not. Be with their sweet baby and their surgeons throughout the surgery and recovery. In Your name we pray, Amen.

THOUGHTS FOR TODAY

DAY 18

Isaiah 26:3 You will keep in perfect peace those whose minds are steadfast, because they trust in You. Trust in the Lord forever, for the Lord, the Lord Himself, is the Rock eternal.

He's got the mom who feels robbed of kicks in His hands. This mama had her baby much earlier than expected and feels like she missed out on lots of flutters and kicks. I find it hard to explain to people that don't have preemies. The answer I always get is "yeah, but you got to hold her sooner!" Yes, I got to hold her sooner, but I held her while she couldn't breathe without help and had lots of tubes and wires connected. I missed out on 13 weeks of kicks. Kicks that would assure me she was okay. All of this to say, it's okay to feel robbed even when no one else understands it.

Dear Lord, this mama feels like she missed out on feeling little kicks and movements because her baby came early. To be honest Lord, this is something I still struggle with. Be with us and give us peace, trusting that this is all in Your plan, and You are working all things for our good. In Your name we pray, Amen.

THOUGHTS FOR TODAY

DAY 19

Isaiah 40:30-31 Even youths grow tired and weary, and young men stumble and fall; but those who hope in the Lord will renew their strength. They will soar on wings like eagles; they will run and not grow weary, they will walk and not be faint.

He's got the mama whose baby is getting more caffeine than she is in His hands. This baby needs caffeine to keep their heart beating and their lungs breathing. And this mama feels the same way. If someone offered this mama straight caffeine in a syringe, she'd surely take it. She's barely making it on the iced coffee she had this morning. I would joke with our nurses and ask if they had any extra for me after giving it to my daughter.

Dear Lord, this mama needs the type of energy only You can provide. She is a new kind of tired and needs an infusion of caffeine just like her sweet baby. We ask that You'll give her energy and strength today and multiply her rest tonight. In Your name we pray, Amen.

THOUGHTS FOR TODAY

DAY 20

Psalm 41:3 The Lord sustains them on their sickbed and restores them from their bed of illness.

He's got the baby with NEC in His hands. NEC is such a big deal in the NICU. I feel like it was talked about from day one: what it was and how to avoid it. It was always in the back of my mind. Unfortunately, even after doing everything right, my daughter ended up with medical NEC. Thankfully she didn't need surgery, but lots of babies do! Let's pray for strength for these babies.

Dear Lord, NEC is so scary. We pray that You'll comfort the parents of these babies and give them a sense of peace that only You can provide. Heal these little babies and give them strength to pull through it. Sustain them and restore them from their illness, Lord. In Your name we pray, Amen.

THOUGHTS FOR TODAY

DAY 21

Ephesians 1:7 In Him we have redemption through His blood, the forgiveness of sins, in accordance with the riches of God's grace

He's got the baby who needs a blood transfusion in His hands. This baby is declining, and it's been decided that they need blood. Hearing "blood transfusion" come from the doctors is so scary. At least for me it was. I was terrified the first time my baby got blood. However, once I saw what a difference it made in her, I wasn't scared the next few times. Maybe this prayer is more for the parents than the baby!

Dear Lord, we thank You for the person that donated blood so that our babies can thrive. Be with this baby and help their body to accept the blood safely. Lord, we also ask that You'll be with these parents that are worried about the transfusion. Give them peace, Lord. In Your name we pray, Amen.

THOUGHTS FOR TODAY

DAY 22

Ephesians 5:25 Husbands, love your wives, just as Christ loved the church and gave Himself up for her.

He's got the dad that takes care of Mama in His hands. This dad is an amazing partner. He is helping mama as she continues to heal from the delivery. He may be helping her to the bathroom, helping her change clothes, or washing pump parts. This dad is going above and beyond to do everything he can to make this easier, mentally and physically on Mama.

Dear Lord, thank You for the men that are wonderful partners and fathers. Healing from a delivery is tough, and his help has been priceless. Guide him to know how to help, Lord. Give him strength so he may continue to do so. In Your name we pray, Amen.

THOUGHTS FOR TODAY

DAY 23

Psalms 27:14 Wait patiently for the Lord. Be brave and courageous. Yes, wait patiently for the Lord.

He's got the parents who can't hold their baby in His hands. This mama and dad long to hold their baby. Whether baby is a day old or a month old, it's killing them that they can't hold their littlest love. My daughter was 2 days old when I first held her, and I know how blessed I was for that. There's this expectation that you have of holding your sweet baby right after you deliver and for most NICU parents that doesn't happen. We pray for the parents that can't hold their babies today.

Dear Lord, we know this mama and dad long to hold their baby. Things didn't go the way they expected, and they didn't get to hold their baby right after birth. Please hold them and their sweet baby in Your arms today, Lord. In Your name we pray, Amen.

THOUGHTS FOR TODAY

DAY 24

Genesis 2:7 And the Lord God formed man of the dust of the ground and breathed air into his nostrils the breath of life; and man became a living soul.

He's got the respiratory baby in His hands. This baby is on the ventilator, CPAP, or high flow oxygen and is struggling to breathe on their own. My baby went from CPAP, to room air, to oxygen, back to CPAP, and then back to room air. Going back to CPAP seemed like such a step back, but it was necessary. I had to trust in His plan.

Dear Lord, be with this baby and help them to breathe easier. We ask that You will breathe the breath of life into them and heal their lungs. Be with all of the parents of these babies and assure them that even when it seems like a setback, it is still in Your plan. In Your name we pray, Amen.

THOUGHTS FOR TODAY

DAY 25

Philippians 4:19 And this same God who takes care of me will supply all your needs from His glorious riches, which have been given to us in Christ Jesus.

He's got the family that's struggling financially in His hands. A NICU stay is no small thing when it comes to finances. The bills can make a huge impact. Not only that but buying lunch daily, the gas to get there and back, and entertaining big siblings at the zoo, aquarium, or museum. A lot more can go into a NICU stay than many people may realize. Financial strain is hard on any relationship, including your relationship with the Lord.

Dear Lord, please be with this family who is in the NICU. A NICU journey is hard enough without having to worry about the financial burden it brings along with it. Give this family peace knowing that you will provide and make a way. In Your name we pray, Amen.

THOUGHTS FOR TODAY

DAY 26

Proverbs 31:13 She works willingly with her hands.

He's got all the therapy providers in his hands. The physical therapists, occupational therapists, and speech language pathologists. These lovely people are instrumental in many NICU journeys, and I think they often get overlooked. They help our babies meet milestones that get them home! For us, it was our occupational therapist, Torey, who made a huge impact. She helped my baby learn to take her bottles and helped me by giving me the confidence to advocate for my baby.

Dear Lord, we thank You for the people that were called to help our babies. Making sure their bodies continue to develop as they should and helping them learn to eat is a big part of getting home, and we couldn't do it without them. Guide their thoughts and actions as they care for our babies. In Your name we pray, Amen.

THOUGHTS FOR TODAY

DAY 27

Psalms 73:23-24 Yet I am always with You; You hold me by my right hand. You guide me with Your counsel, and afterward You will take me into glory.

He's got the mom that feels alone in His hands. It is so easy to feel alone, even surrounded by people walking similar journeys. Even if Dad is there or maybe other family, none of them quite understand what you're going through. It's different being the mama. Either my husband or my mom was with me at all times. I was very rarely actually alone but was still lonely. But we're never truly alone. The Lord our God walks with us through this journey and is there for us to lean on. Don't forget that.

Dear Lord, even full of people, the NICU can be a lonely place. You feel alone in your thoughts. The "what ifs" and "now whats". Remind this mama that You are always with her for her to lean on and to voice her concerns to You Lord. In your name we pray, Amen.

THOUGHTS FOR TODAY

DAY 28

Psalms 9:9-10 The Lord is a refuge for the oppressed, a stronghold in times of trouble. Those who know Your name trust in You, for You, Lord, have never forsaken those who seek You.

He's got the parents whose relationship is struggling in His hands. These parents are going through so much and their relationship or marriage is struggling. There are so many decisions to be made that they may not agree on. They may not be handling this journey the same way emotionally, which is making things harder. They just aren't sure how to get back to where they were.

Dear Lord, we thank You for the relationships we have with our partners. We pray that You will help us get through this together. Help these parents to trust in You as they work through this journey. In Your name we pray, Amen.

THOUGHTS FOR TODAY

DAY 29

Psalms 42:5 Why are you cast down, O my soul, and why are you in turmoil within me? Hope in God; for I shall again praise Him, my salvation.

He's got the mama who struggles with prayer in His hands. Yes mama, you too! The Lord is holding you and your baby in His hands through this journey. Lean on Him when you feel tired. Lean on Him when you have nothing else to give. For a while after I had my baby, I struggled to pray because I didn't understand why things happened the way they did. I wasn't necessarily mad at Him. I just didn't understand so I didn't know what to say. Even when you aren't sure what to say, just spend time with Him. He knows your heart. He knows what you need before you even ask.

Dear Lord, be with this mama today. Let her know that all she needs to do is ask. Lord, hold this mama in Your hands. We ask that You will guide her words as she prays. In Your name we pray, Amen.

THOUGHTS FOR TODAY

DAY 30

Psalms 23:4 Even though I walk through the darkest valley, I will fear no evil for You are with me; Your rod and Your staff they comfort me.

He's got the security guards in His hands. This may seem like an odd group to include, but I was so thankful for them so many times. There were multiple nights that I stayed very late-into the wee hours of the morning-and getting to my car was scary. The security guards were so helpful and saved me from some interesting encounters more than once. Next time you see hospital security, tell them thank you!

Dear Lord, we thank You for the guards that keep us safe around the hospital. There are lots of moms coming and going from the NICU that appreciate having someone to look out for them. Lord, we ask that You'll keep them safe as they keep us safe. In Your name we pray, Amen.

THOUGHTS FOR TODAY

DAY 31

Psalms 34:17-18 The righteous cry out, and the Lord hears them; He delivers them from all their troubles. The Lord is close to the broken hearted and saves those who are crushed in spirit.

He's got the mom who's had losses in His hands. This mama lost one or more pregnancies before her sweet rainbow baby arrived. Now her rainbow baby needs the NICU, and she is terrified of what may happen. I see you mama and I pray for you.

Dear Lord, this mama has been through so much already. She's stronger than she knows. Be close to her and hear her as she cries out, Lord. We ask that You hold her and comfort her. Give her a sense of peace that only You can provide. In Your name we pray, Amen.

THOUGHTS FOR TODAY

DAY 32

Jeremiah 30:17 "But I will restore you to health and heal your wounds" declares the Lord.

He's got the babies with a brain bleed in His hands. Like most things in the NICU, brain bleeds are scary. They can affect so much like growth and development. Even though this is something we didn't experience on our journey, I pray for everyone who has.

Dear Lord, thank You for the blessing of our sweet babies. We ask that You heal their little brains. Shrink any bleeds already there and prevent any more from forming. Heal them of any lasting effects from the bleeds, Lord. Give these babies strength to fight. In Your name we pray, Amen.

THOUGHTS FOR TODAY

DAY 33

Ecclesiastes 4:9-10a Two are better than one, because they have a good return for their labor: If either of them falls down, one can help the other up.

He's got your NICU mom friend in His hands. I hope you've made a friend with another mom in your NICU. Maybe your roomie, your pod mate, or just a mom you met in the family room. Either way, it is so refreshing to have someone who knows what you are going through, someone to talk to that understands all the NICU jargon and all the small victories. We had a few roomies but one in particular, Macy, was such a blessing to us and our journey! You could see and feel her love for Jesus just by talking to her. When you find your mom friend, start a conversation about God and your church. Tell her what He's done for you! Maybe she knows Christ as her Savior, and if she doesn't you may just change her life by telling her what He's done for you and that He can do the same for her.

Dear Lord, we thank You for the other moms in the NICU that have become our friends. It is such a blessing to have someone to lean on that is on a similar journey. Help us to be good friends to them and to support them as much as they've supported us. We pray that whether they know You yet or not, that this NICU journey will help them to grow in their relationship with You. In Your name we pray, Amen.

THOUGHTS FOR TODAY

DAY 34

Job 33:4 The Spirit of God has made me; the breath of the Almighty gives me life.

He's got the respiratory therapists in His hands. The wonderful people who keep lots of our babies breathing well! Whether your baby is intubated, on CPAP, or just high flow oxygen, a respiratory therapist cares for your baby. They can play a much larger role when a baby is going home on a ventilator or with a trach. They help train these parents how to care for their baby on their own at home. Let's pray for them.

Dear Lord, we thank You for the respiratory therapists caring for our babies. We pray that You'll guide their decisions and their hands as they do so. In Your name we pray, Amen.

THOUGHTS FOR TODAY

DAY 35

Isaiah 43:18-19 Forget the former things; do not dwell on the past. See, I am doing a new thing! Now it springs up; do you not perceive it? I am making a way in the wilderness and streams in the wasteland.

He's got the mama who feels stuck in His hands. Stuck because her baby is still intubated. Stuck because her baby got sick. Stuck because the NICU is one step forward and two steps back. I remember this feeling all too well. Just a feeling of helplessness. "She'll go home when she's ready" was my least favorite thing to hear, but I knew I couldn't rush things. Let's pray together.

Dear Lord, we pray for this mama who feels stuck in the NICU. Things are moving slowly. We pray she knows that this journey is moving at exactly the pace it should because You have it all under control. Give her the understanding to know You've got this. In Your name we pray, Amen.

THOUGHTS FOR TODAY

DAY 36

Matthew 4:4 "It is written: 'Man shall not live on bread alone, but on every word that comes from the mouth of God.'"

He's got the baby who is struggling to eat in His hands. There are so many reasons a baby could be struggling to eat: age or immaturity, swallowing problems, intestinal issues, a recent surgery, the list goes on and on. Figuring out how to get baby's nutrition in is crucial when it comes to going home. The last several weeks of our NICU journey were just waiting on her to be able to finish her bottles. The waiting was so hard! Your baby may just need time, feeding therapy, an NG tube or a G tube. Whatever the case, they are in His hands.

Dear Lord, we pray for the baby that can't eat right now. We pray that the medical professionals working with this baby will help figure out how to get their nutrition in. We pray that You'll give this baby the strength they need to learn to eat in whatever way they can. Please give these parents the patience they need as they wait to go home. Be with this whole family today, Lord. In Your name we pray, Amen.

THOUGHTS FOR TODAY

DAY 37

Galatians 6:9 Let us not become weary in doing good, for at the proper time we will reap a harvest if we do not give up.

He's got the mama without a village in His hands. "It takes a village," they say. Well, what if you don't have one? I had a heck of a village and can't imagine doing it without one. I look up to the mamas that do it on their own. My only question is-how?! How do you do it? Bravo!

Dear Lord, today we pray for the mama without a village. She's doing this with just the baby's father's help or maybe none at all! She's amazingly strong and unbelievably tired. Lord, we ask that You multiply her rest and renew her strength for the coming days. In Your name we pray, Amen.

THOUGHTS FOR TODAY

DAY 38

Mark 10:14b-15 "Let the little children come to me, and do not hinder them, for the kingdom of God belongs to such as these. Truly I tell you, anyone who will not receive the kingdom of God like a little child will never enter it."

He's got the loved one playing with your kids in His hands. The one playing with the most random toy like a pool noodle. The one running up and down the tiny hall screaming "1-2-3-YAY!". The loved one spending all of their energy entertaining your biggest babies. For us, it was my mom "Momo", when she wasn't with her daddy. Momo played endlessly and never said no to whatever my daughter wanted to do. I truly couldn't have done it without her. I was able to stay in the NICU with baby as long as I needed, without feeling guilty, because I knew my big girl was having fun with Momo. Thank you, Momma.

Dear Lord, we thank You for the people You've blessed our kids with. We are always thankful for them, but this NICU journey makes us realize it a little more. Bless them, Lord, and renew their strength to give them energy to keep playing, Lord. In Your name we pray, Amen.

THOUGHTS FOR TODAY

DAY 39

Psalm 73:26 My flesh and my heart may fail, but God is the strength of my heart and my portion forever.

He's got the baby with heart problems in His hands. This could be something as "small" as a hole in the heart or something as big as needing a transplant. No matter the problem, this baby is in His hands. I know that even the "smallest" problems can seem big. My daughter had two holes in her heart which was very scary at the time. We are still dealing with one of them, and I am thankful it was not something more.

Dear Lord, we pray for the baby who has problems with their heart. No matter what the problem is, we know You have it under control. Heal this baby's heart. Be with the medical professionals handling this problem and guide their actions and decisions, please Lord. In Your name we pray, Amen.

THOUGHTS FOR TODAY

DAY 40

1 Corinthians 14:33 (ESV) For God is not a God of confusion but of peace—as in all the congregations of the Lord's people.

He's got the parents with a language barrier in His hands. A NICU journey is such a hard thing to go through. It can be hard to understand what the doctors and nurses are saying even in your native language. I can't imagine the confusion and worry when they are speaking a different language. Thankfully, there are interpreting services, but I am sure they still leave some questions unanswered.

Dear Lord, we pray for the parents who speak a different language than the doctors and nurses. We pray that You will help to bridge the gap that they feel and assure them that their baby is under the best care no matter the language spoken. In Your name we pray, Amen.

THOUGHTS FOR TODAY

DAY 41

1 Peter 5:6-7 Humble yourselves, therefore, under God's mighty hand, that He may lift you up in due time. Cast all your anxiety on Him because He cares for you.

He's got the dad that feels alone in His hands. This dad may or may not be able to stay at the NICU daily. Regardless, he feels alone. No one quite understands what he's going through. The mom is there for him to talk to, but he feels bad because she is already going through so much herself.

Dear Lord, we ask that You hold this dad in Your hands today. He feels alone and doesn't know how to fix it. He doesn't have a way to help mom or baby which makes him feel even more isolated. Comfort him and assure him that being there for them is all they need. Be there for Him, Lord, as You always are. In Your name we pray, Amen.

THOUGHTS FOR TODAY

DAY 42

Romans 5:3-4 Not only so, but we also glory in our sufferings, because we know that suffering produces perseverance, perseverance, character; and character, hope.

He's got the mom who can't nurse in His hands. This mama wants to nurse her baby so badly, but something isn't going their way. Baby won't latch, baby stops breathing while nursing, or maybe her letdown is too much for baby. No matter the reason, it's hard for this mama to accept. I was this mama. I breastfed my first daughter and planned to do the same with our second. She nursed for a while, but the NICU pushed bottles because it was easier to track her intake. So, I went with it. By the time we got home, she wanted nothing to do with nursing. So, I exclusively pumped. It's hard when things don't go the way you planned. Very little does in the NICU, but that's okay because it's all God's will.

Dear Lord, this mama wanted to be able to nurse her baby, but it was not meant to be. Help this mama to understand and accept Your plan for her and her baby. May she find comfort knowing that they are in Your hands. In Your name we pray, Amen.

THOUGHTS FOR TODAY

DAY 43

Psalm 27:10 Though my father and mother forsake me, the Lord will receive me.

Deuteronomy 31:8 The Lord himself goes before you and will be with you; He will never leave you nor forsake you. Do not be afraid; do not be discouraged.

He's got the baby without people, in His hands. This baby doesn't have anyone. Mama came in alone, had this baby, and left afterwards. No one has been back. This baby will end up in the system, hopefully, in a loving home. The nurses and volunteers are the only ones to hold this baby, and of course the Lord holds them in His hands.

Dear Lord, this baby has no one but You right now. The nurses and volunteers can only do so much. Be with them as they hold this sweet baby. We ask that You place this baby into a loving home and always let them know how much they are loved. In Your name we pray, Amen.

THOUGHTS FOR TODAY

DAY 44

Matthew 11:28 Come to me, all you who are weary and burdened, and I will give you rest.

He's got the beyond tired mama in His hands. The mama who is struggling to even care for herself. The mama who can't sleep because when she closes her eyes, she hears her baby's alarms and replays the worst days. The mama who is up every 3 hours to pump at night. The mama who is barely hanging on but has to for her other kids. It's a tired that you can't describe to someone who hasn't lived it. Only God can supply the strength that it takes to push through this kind of tired. Let's pray for that supernatural strength.

Dear Lord, this mama is TIRED. Let her know that You see her. You see how hard she is pushing through for her family. Lord, this mama needs the kind of strength that only You can provide. Help her to keep pushing through this incredible journey with her baby. In Your name we pray, Amen.

THOUGHTS FOR TODAY

DAY 45

Proverbs 27:17 As iron sharpens iron, so one person sharpens another.

He's got your special person in his hands. Whether it is a medical assistant, nurse, doctor, or someone else. I hope you have a person in your journey that makes it better. If you haven't found that person yet, don't worry, you will. Ours was our dietician, Agnes. She was the light of our journey and made a huge difference for our baby as well as for me personally. Let's thank God for these people.

Dear Lord, thank You for providing someone to light up our journeys. We pray that if there is someone reading this who hasn't found their person yet, that You'll send them soon! Keep this person safe and let them know how loved they are-by this baby's family and by You. In Your name we pray, Amen.

THOUGHTS FOR TODAY

DAY 46

John 1:12-13 Yet to all who did receive Him, to those who believed in His name, He gave the right to become children of God—children born not of natural descent, nor of human decision or a husband's will, but born of God.

He's got the mom who has lost herself in His hands. It is so easy to lose yourself after having a baby even without a NICU journey. Adding the NICU to the mix, makes it even easier. Everything is about baby, as it should be. But, trying to juggle baby and everything going on with them, along with everyday life with your family and friends, there is no time for yourself. No time for the hobbies you used to love or even a little self-care. Please try to take time for yourself.

Dear Lord, we pray for the mama that is struggling to find herself again. She's lost herself somewhere between the NICU and home. We ask that You hold her and assure her that You know exactly who she is, Your beloved daughter. Give her time to care for herself, do something she enjoys, and rest in You Lord. In Your name we pray, Amen.

THOUGHTS FOR TODAY

DAY 47

1 Peter 5:10 And the God of all grace, who called you to His eternal glory in Christ, after you have suffered a little while, will Himself restore you and make you strong, firm, and steadfast.

He's got the baby with reflux in His hands. Reflux causes so many problems and is hard to treat when they are so little. It can feel so aggravating and defeating. My daughter's reflux was the main cause of her bradycardia and desaturation episodes, and there was nothing they could do for the reflux. I felt so helpless, and I could tell it made her miserable. Let's pray for these sweet babies.

Dear Lord, these poor babies with reflux are miserable. It makes it hard for them to eat and to evem stay stable. Please be with them and heal their reflux today. Guide the doctors and nurses to better help this baby and give this mama peace knowing that she's doing everything she can for her baby. In Your name we pray, Amen.

THOUGHTS FOR TODAY

DAY 48

Proverbs 20:24 A person's steps are directed by the Lord. How then can anyone understand their own way?

He's got the mom who had a birth plan in His hands. This mama had everything planned out. Everything she wanted and didn't want when it came to her birth. Lots of mamas who have NICU babies don't get to use their birth plan. I certainly didn't. An emergent c-section at 27 weeks pregnant was definitely not my plan. But it was God's and it got my sweet baby out in the safest way possible.

Dear Lord, thank You for getting our babies here safely, even if it wasn't exactly how we planned it. You knew from the day this baby was conceived exactly how they would enter the world, and You were not worried. Comfort this mama today, Lord. In Your name we pray, Amen.

THOUGHTS FOR TODAY

DAY 49

Romans 15:2 Each of us should please our neighbors for their good, to build them up.

He's got the receptionist in his hands. The sweet lady that knows your name, your bed space, and your baby's name. She asks how baby is doing every time she sees you. This receptionist really cares about the babies and parents. Ours was Mrs. Deborah. She goes the extra mile for the parents in her NICU. She brightened many days for me!

Dear Lord, thank You for the sweet receptionists that greet us every day. Thank You for the ones that know us by name. We pray that You'll be with them and renew their joy daily so they can continue to make a difference in the lives of NICU parents. In Your name we pray, Amen.

THOUGHTS FOR TODAY

DAY 50

John 14:27 Peace I leave with you; my peace I give you. I do not give to you as the world gives. Do not let your hearts be troubled and do not be afraid.

He's got the mama who is sick in His hands. Going to see your baby when you are sick is not really an option. Is it allergies? Is it a cold or RSV? It's hard to tell but you can't risk it. There were a few times over our journey that I missed going to see my daughter because of what I'm sure was allergies, but I wouldn't risk it. Not being able to see your baby is so hard, even when you know you are doing the right thing for them.

Dear Lord, we ask that You will be with this mama while she is sick. We ask that You heal her body so she can get back to her baby, Lord. Give her peace knowing that You have her baby in Your hands as well. Help her to rest and take care of herself. In Your name we pray, Amen.

THOUGHTS FOR TODAY

DAY 51

Psalm 139:10 Even there Your hand will guide me, Your right hand will hold me fast.

He's got the baby under lights in His hands. The "tanning bed" as we so lovingly called it. This baby has elevated bilirubin levels and is jaundiced. This happens for a lot of babies, but it can also slow things down. It can slow down their eating, and you can't hold baby as much when they are under the lights. It's hard when holding your little love is all you want to do.

Dear Lord, we ask that You will be with this little baby who is under the lights today. Help to bring their levels down so that Mom and Dad can hold them tomorrow. We ask that You hold this baby in Your loving hands today since we cannot. We ask You to heal this sweet baby Lord. In Your name we pray, Amen.

THOUGHTS FOR TODAY

DAY 52

Proverbs 3:5-6 Trust in the Lord with all your heart and lean not on your own understanding; in all your ways submit to Him, and He will make your paths straight.

He's got the parents who want more kids in His hands. These parents planned on having more kids after this sweet NICU baby, but things have changed. Maybe the delivery of this baby caused mama not to be able to have more kids. Or maybe they are scared of what might happen if they try to have more. Will having more put mama in danger? Would the next baby come even earlier or have the same struggles? Whatever the case, things are now uncertain for these parents.

Dear Lord, these parents were planning to continue growing their family. However, everything that has happened with this baby has changed things. We ask that You hold these parents and give them comfort knowing that nothing is uncertain for You. If they are meant to have more kids, it will happen. If more children is not in Your will for these parents, please be with them as they grieve the future they thought they would have. In Your name we pray, Amen.

THOUGHTS FOR TODAY

DAY 53

Acts 10:2 He and all his family were devout and God-fearing; he gave generously to those in need and prayed to God regularly.

He's got the baby's aunts and uncles in His hands. The ones that are there for you and your baby. They want to be there physically, but maybe they can't due to distance or hospital regulations. These aunts and uncles likely haven't gotten to hold their sweet niece or nephew yet, but they love them just the same. My sister-in-law is one of my best friends, and I was so thankful to have someone to talk to. Someone that wasn't a doctor or nurse but wasn't my husband or mom either. We are so thankful for our Aunt A and Uncle R.

Dear Lord, we thank You for the support of the baby's aunts and uncles. They are invaluable when it comes to supporting us during this journey. Guide them on how to help us through this. Whether it be an ear to listen or providing some comedic relief along the way. Hold them in Your hands, Lord. In Your name we pray, Amen.

THOUGHTS FOR TODAY

DAY 54

Psalm 147:3 He heals the brokenhearted and binds up their wounds

He's got the mom who missed her baby shower in His hands. Maybe this mama was on strict bed rest, or maybe baby came too early for mom to have a shower. Whatever the case, this mama was looking forward to her baby shower and never got to have it. I had my baby girl the week before I was supposed to have my shower. I hate I missed it, not because of the gifts, but because I wanted to see everyone! You are allowed to be sad about not having a shower!

Dear Lord, we thank You for our sweet babies. We planned to celebrate them with a shower, but that didn't get to happen. Hold this mama and allow her to be upset about what she has missed while still being grateful for what she has. In Your name we pray, Amen.

THOUGHTS FOR TODAY

DAY 55

1 Peter 4:10 Each of you should use whatever gift you have received to serve others, as faithful stewards of God's grace in its various forms.

He's got all the volunteers in His hands. The volunteers at our hospital did so many things. They held babies, made blankets and hats, and even took professional quality pictures of you and baby. It's the little things like that that can make your day.

Dear Lord, we thank You for the wonderful volunteers at our hospitals. There is so much that they help with, and they can make such an impact on the parents' and babies' lives. We ask that You'll guide them to do whatever they can to help, Lord. In Your name we pray, Amen.

THOUGHTS FOR TODAY

DAY 56

1 Thessalonians 1:3 We remember before our God and Father your work produced by faith, your labor prompted by love, and your endurance inspired by hope in our Lord Jesus Christ.

He's got the mama struggling with her milk supply in His hands. Breastfeeding and pumping are such labors of love. To struggle with a low supply can be so frustrating and having an oversupply can feel like such a burden. Both require constantly pumping but for different reasons. One mama is trying to build her supply, and the other mama has to pump so often to stay comfortable and avoid mastitis. Whatever the case, He sees how hard you are working to feed your sweet baby. Trust that He will help you through it.

Dear Lord, thank You for the ability to feed our baby with our body. This mama is trying so hard to do so. Give her the strength she needs to manage her supply. Nourish her body and multiply her rest to help her provide food for her baby. In Your name we pray, Amen.

THOUGHTS FOR TODAY

DAY 57

Galatians 6:10 Therefore, as we have opportunity, let us do good to all people, especially to those who belong to the family of believers

He's got your whole community in His hands. Family and friends you haven't seen in years, your church family, and the people that you barely know that came out of the woodwork to help. We were so incredibly thankful for our community during our journey. People sent money, gifts and food. Our sweet church family did fundraisers that helped tremendously! What we were most thankful for, though, was the prayers we could feel daily. A big thank you to our community and church family.

Dear Lord, we're so thankful for the community you've surrounded us with. They have been praying since the moment they found out about what this family is going through. Their prayers and support are priceless during this time. We ask that you continue to bless our communities, Lord. In Your name we pray, Amen.

THOUGHTS FOR TODAY

DAY 58

Isaiah 43:19 See, I am doing a new thing! Now it springs up; do you not perceive it? I am making a way in the wilderness and streams in the wasteland.

He's got the baby with big changes coming in His hands. This baby has big plans ahead! They may be coming off of the ventilator or CPAP today. Maybe they are starting to try eating by mouth today. No matter the plans, this baby needs strength to pull through today.

Dear Lord, big things are happening soon! We pray that You will give this baby strength to do what needs to be done today. Sometimes our plans don't work out, and if that is the case today Lord, please be with this baby as well as their parents. Assure the parents that everything is going according to Your will Lord. In Your name we pray, Amen.

THOUGHTS FOR TODAY

DAY 59

Proverbs 27:9 Perfume and incense bring joy to the heart, and the pleasantness of a friend springs from their heartfelt advice.

He's got the mom who misses her friends in His hands. This mama misses her friends, near or far. Being in the NICU takes a lot of your time, whether you are close to home or hundreds of miles away. You could be 5 minutes from a friend's house and not see them because all of your extra time is spent with your sweet baby in the NICU. Lean on these friends for support when you can.

Dear Lord, we thank You for the friends You've blessed us with. We pray that they know that they aren't forgotten; all of our spare time goes to our sweet baby in the NICU. Lord, please encourage these friends to reach out even if they don't know what to say. In Your name we pray, Amen.

THOUGHTS FOR TODAY

DAY 60

1 Peter 3:7 Husbands, in the same way be considerate as you live with your wives, and treat them with respect as the weaker partner and as heirs with you of the gracious gift of life, so that nothing will hinder your prayers.

He's got the dad who feels helpless in His hands. This dad doesn't know how to help his baby. Mom typically does so much in the NICU...Feeding, skin to skin, diaper changes. Dads can absolutely do these things and give bottles, but nurses, a lot of times, gravitate towards the moms for this. He sees how much she enjoys it and would never take that away. He just wishes there was more he could do to help on a daily basis; physically or emotionally.

Dear Lord, thank You for the dads that want to help. Their support is invaluable during this journey. Hold them in Your hands and guide them through this, helping him to help her. In Your name we pray, Amen.

THOUGHTS FOR TODAY

DAY 61

Matthew 19:14 Jesus said, "Let the little children come to me, and do not hinder them, for the kingdom of heaven belongs to such as these."

He's got the child life specialists in His hands. These sweet ladies bring joy into every room. They provide mobiles and toys for the older babies and take care of the big siblings too. Because big sister wasn't allowed in the NICU, our child life specialist made a picture book explaining everything in baby's room. She also made her a baby doll that had all of the same tubes and wires attached to it that our baby did. The baby doll had lead stickers and wires, a pulse oximeter on her foot, a feeding tube, and a CPAP mask. She made a huge difference in big sister's journey.

Dear Lord, we thank You for the kind souls that care for our babies, big and small. Long NICU stays can be hard on baby as well as on their big siblings. Please guide the child life specialists as they work to make everyone's journey easier. In Your name we pray, Amen.

THOUGHTS FOR TODAY

DAY 62

Genesis 1:26 Then God said, "Let us make mankind in our image, in our likeness, so that they may rule over the fish in the sea and the birds in the sky, over the livestock and all the wild animals, and over all the creatures that move along the ground."

He's got your fur babies at home in His hands. Laugh if you want but my pets were my first babies and their lives have definitely changed since being in the NICU. Whether you are home every night or hundreds of miles away, your pets know something is going on. Give them some extra love the next time you see them.

Dear Lord, those of us with pets love them dearly and they are going through changes as well. Be with them and let them know they are still so loved. We ask that you'll also be with us as we miss our fur babies. In Your name we pray, Amen.

THOUGHTS FOR TODAY

DAY 63

Psalm 56:3 When I am afraid, I put my trust in You.

He's got the baby that's been exposed to sickness in His hands. This baby was exposed to someone who was sick and is now at risk of getting sick themselves. This is a scary time for the parents. Our daughter was exposed to Covid during her NICU stay. Thankfully she never caught it, but the quarantine was very scary. Anyone that went in her room had to be gowned and masked. It was so unsettling.

Dear Lord, we pray for the baby who was exposed to a sickness. We pray that You will be with them and give them strength to pull through this if they get sick. We pray that You will be with the parents who are so scared right now. Help them to trust in You Lord. In Your name we pray, Amen.

THOUGHTS FOR TODAY

DAY 64

Psalm 22:9 Yet You brought me out of the womb; You made me trust in You, even at my mother's breast

He's got the lactation consultants in His hands. These ladies have their work cut out for them with all the pumping mamas! They help ease the stress of learning to pump for a preemie as well as helping moms start to nurse. The loving comfort they provide is just what lots of moms need.

Dear Lord, we are so thankful for the lactation consultants that help us learn to feed our babies with our bodies, whether that's through pumping or nursing. We ask that You'll guide them to help each mom in whatever way she needs, Lord. In Your name we pray, Amen.

THOUGHTS FOR TODAY

DAY 65

Matthew 28:20b And surely I am with you always, to the very end of the age.

He's got the mama who can't physically be there in His hands. This mama had to go back to work to provide for her family. She wants so badly to be in the NICU holding her baby. Don't feel guilty Mama. That baby knows how loved they are!

Dear Lord, this mama misses her baby while she is at work. She longs to be there holding her little love. Be with her today and hold her in Your hands Lord. We ask that You comfort her and assure her that You have her baby in Your hands too. In Your name we pray, Amen.

THOUGHTS FOR TODAY

DAY 66

Psalm 51:7 Cleanse me with hyssop and I will be clean; wash me, and I will be whiter than snow.

He's got the housekeeping ladies in His hands. These ladies keep our babies' spaces clean and tidy. The ladies that come in and make small talk and say they'll pray for your baby. We were so thankful for our cleaning ladies, and the sweet lady that came and restocked the room every day. I wish I could remember her name, so I could thank her properly.

Dear Lord, thank You for the ladies that keep our babies' spaces cleaned and stocked. A clean and functional space makes things just a little bit easier. We pray that You will be with these ladies and give them strength to continue helping babies. In Your name we pray, Amen.

THOUGHTS FOR TODAY

DAY 67

Psalms 62:1 Truly my soul finds rest in God; my salvation comes from Him.

He's got the mom of multiples in His hands. Twins, triplets, quadruplets or more. This mama doesn't just have one baby in the NICU, she's got multiple. I can't imagine the emotions she goes through on a daily basis. Happiness when one baby has a success while worrying until the other(s) do the same. Extra worry, but hopefully extra happiness too.

Dear Lord, this mama has so much going on with multiple babies in the NICU. Assure her that while she is overwhelmed, You are not. You gave her these babies because You knew she could handle it. I ask that You'll multiply her rest today and renew her strength, Lord. In Your name we pray, Amen.

THOUGHTS FOR TODAY

DAY 68

2 Corinthians 9:8 And God is able to bless you abundantly, so that in all things at all times, having all that you need, you will abound in every good work.

He's got the parents who are out of work in His hands. One or both of these parents aren't able to work right now. This was me. I got put on bed rest at 13 weeks pregnant and didn't return to work until after our 80 days in the NICU. I was out of work for 8 months. This is hard emotionally as well as financially. Feeling like you can't do much to help your family is so hard.

Dear Lord, we pray for any parents that are out of work right now. No matter the situation, it's hard to feel like you can't help provide for your family. It is quite the financial burden. Please be with these parents, Lord. Help them to cope and to trust in You to provide for their needs, Lord. In Your name we pray, Amen.

THOUGHTS FOR TODAY

DAY 69

Psalm 55:22 Cast your cares on the Lord and He will sustain you; He will never let the righteous be shaken.

He's got the dad at home with big siblings in His hands. This dad is happy to do his part and is doing so much at home by himself. He's doing big sister's hair for the first time-pig tails are hard! He's getting them ready for school, doing drop off and pickup, ball practice and dance classes. He's got homework and supper and maybe sometimes bath time and bed. He is stressed starting and ending the day but is comforted knowing he's in the hands of the true Provider.

Dear Lord, we are so thankful for the dads that do their part. We pray for the dads who are at home juggling big siblings and everything that goes with them. He needs strength to continue on. Please be with him and multiply his rest tonight, Lord, In Your name we pray, Amen.

THOUGHTS FOR TODAY

DAY 70

Ecclesiastes 3:1 There is a time for everything and a season for every activity under the heavens.

He's got the parents who are out of patience in His hands. These parents did not expect to be in the NICU this long. Maybe baby was full term or at least close to it. This NICU journey was expected to be short and sweet, but they hit a bump in the road, and now they are still here. These parents don't know how much longer they'll be here and are beyond ready to be home.

Dear Lord, we pray for the parents that weren't expecting this long of a NICU stay. We pray that You will give them the extra patience they need to make it through. Assure them that everything is happening in Your time Lord. In Your name we pray, Amen.

THOUGHTS FOR TODAY

DAY 71

Proverbs 23:18 There is surely a future hope for you, and your hope will not be cut off

He's got the family that is dreaming of going home in His hands. Their baby only has one thing left to conquer. They may need to finish their bottles or just to stop having Brady episodes. Whatever it is, they are so close to going home. Close enough to start dreaming about it at least.

Dear Lord, this sweet family can see the light at the end of the tunnel. If they aren't going home as soon as they would hope, we ask that You give them patience as they wait until the day comes. Give them strength to make it through this last stretch, Lord. In Your name we pray, Amen.

THOUGHTS FOR TODAY

DAY 72

Proverbs 16:3 Commit to the Lord whatever you do, and He will establish your plans.

He's got the dad working on the nursery in His hands. His baby came earlier than expected, and the nursery isn't ready yet! There's a crib to build, a closet to fill, and decorations to hang. Our nursery wouldn't have gotten done in time if it wasn't for my husband and his mom! Honestly, as long as there is a safe place to sleep, food, clothes, and diapers the baby will be just fine until the nursery is ready.

Dear Lord, please be with this dad as he prepares a place for his sweet baby. Ease his mind that everything will be fine if everything isn't just so. Give him the strength to get everything together and the patience to get it all done. In Your name we pray, Amen.

THOUGHTS FOR TODAY

DAY 73

James 1:2-3 Consider it pure joy, my brothers and sisters, whenever you face trials of many kinds, because you know that the testing of your faith produces perseverance.

He's got the family leaving with equipment in His hands. This family will be going home soon with medical equipment in tow. They may be going home with a feeding tube, oxygen, or a ventilator. They are excited about going home but didn't originally expect equipment. These parents are learning new procedures and techniques to care for their baby once they get home. It can't be easy.

Dear Lord, thank You for the opportunity for this family to go home, even if it is not how they imagined. Please be with the parents as they learn everything they need to know about bringing their baby home. Please be with the baby and give them strength to endure this transition from NICU to home. In Your name we pray, Amen.

THOUGHTS FOR TODAY

DAY 74

Psalm 37:7 Be still before the Lord and wait patiently for Him; do not fret when people succeed in their ways, when they carry out their wicked schemes.

He's got the family who is staying in His hands. This family is not going home just yet. They've watched countless babies around them going home, but their baby isn't ready yet and that's okay. These parents would never rush their baby's progress, but it is so hard to watch others go home while they stay.

Dear Lord, please be with this family as they accept that it is not their time to go home yet. They are beyond ready to be home with their sweet baby and start their life as a family. Lord, please give them patience and comfort as they wait for their turn. Assure them that this is all happening according to Your will. In Your name we pray, Amen.

THOUGHTS FOR TODAY

DAY 75

Lamentations 3:22-23 Because of the Lord's great love we are not consumed, for His compassions never fail. They are new every morning; great is Your faithfulness.

He's got the family that's going home, in His hands. FINALLY! This family is so happy to be going home but they are also so nervous. What if something happens at home? This has been such a journey! Now, going home starts a beautiful new journey for this sweet family.

Dear Lord, thank You for Your faithfulness. The journey this family has been on has been hard, and now, they are going home with their baby. Please keep this baby healthy at home. Give these parents a sense of peace knowing that You have everything under control. In Your name we pray, Amen.

THOUGHTS FOR TODAY

DAY 76

Mark 11:24 Therefore I tell you, whatever you ask for in prayer, believe that you have received it, and it will be yours.

He's got your first night at home in His hands. You are finally home-enjoy it! I know it can be scary, but this is what you've been waiting on. The doctors wouldn't have sent baby home if they weren't sure they were ready. Soak up all the snuggles in the comfort of your own home.

Dear Lord, this family is finally home! Thank You for getting them here. Please be with them and give them the strength they need to get through this change. We pray that everyone is able to rest tonight and wake refreshed for their first full day at home tomorrow. In Your name we pray, Amen.

THOUGHTS FOR TODAY

DAY 77

Philippians 4:7 And the peace of God, which transcends all understanding will guard your hearts and your minds in Christ Jesus.

He's got the big siblings in His hands. Now, baby is home, and this is a whole new journey for them. Maybe they had just gotten used to how things were with baby in the NICU, and now this is so different. Now, they are splitting attention at home with the new baby. At least this is something all siblings go through-having baby come home. As you've figured out, your love multiplies, not divides. Now they are finally all under the same roof!

Dear Lord, we are so thankful for the big siblings that are starting a new journey with baby at home. We ask that You will be with them and give them the understanding that Mom and Dad still love them just ask much, and now their love can multiply too. In Your name we pray, Amen.

THOUGHTS FOR TODAY

DAY 78

Psalm 118:8 It is better to take refuge in the Lord than to trust in humans.

He's got all the specialists in His hands. All of the follow-up appointments with specialists can be overwhelming. Cardiology, neurology, GI, the list goes on and on. It can be even more nerve wrecking if these aren't the same specialists that took care of your baby in the NICU. Now you have to learn to trust a whole new team of doctors. Trusting them can be hard, but what matters is that you trust in the Lord.

Dear Lord, there can be so many follow up appointments to keep up with after leaving the NICU. Sometimes it is all just too much. We pray that You'll hold these specialists in Your hands and guide them as they care for our babies outside of the NICU. In Your name we pray, Amen.

THOUGHTS FOR TODAY

DAY 79

Philippians 4:9 Whatever you have learned or received or heard from me or seen in me—put into practice. And the God of peace will be with you.

He's got the family that's finding a new normal in His hands. Finding a new normal is hard no matter if you spent 2 days or 300 days in the NICU. I imagine its harder with multiple siblings or with medical equipment sent home. Don't worry, you will eventually find a new routine that works for you, try not to rush it.

Dear Lord, we are so thankful for the families that are home now. We thank You for this life of ours. We pray that You will be with them and help them to find their new normal. Give them the patience to find their new routine and figure out what works and what doesn't. In Your name we pray, Amen.

THOUGHTS FOR TODAY

DAY 80

Psalms 95:4-5 In His hand are the depths of the earth, and the mountain peaks belong to Him. The sea is His, for He made it, and His hands formed the dry land.

He's got the whole world in His hands. He's got everything you are worried about in His hands. He's got the world you are nervous to raise your children in, in His hands. He's got you and me sister, in His hands. Whether you are reading this last day at home or still in the NICU; He's got you!

Dear Lord, I thank you for the lovely people reading this book. I thank You for their sweet baby, and the journey You've given them. Please be with them on whatever journey they are currently on, whether that is at home or in the NICU. I pray that You will give them strength and joy, Lord. In Your name I pray, Amen.

Made in the USA
Monee, IL
24 March 2025